BODY IMAGE

Self-Acceptance vs. Imperfection

by

Deshireé Capri King

PublishAmerica
Baltimore

© 2008 by Desireé Capri King.
All rights reserved. No part of this book may be reproduced, stored in a retrieval system or transmitted in any form or by any means without the prior written permission of the publishers, except by a reviewer who may quote brief passages in a review to be printed in a newspaper, magazine or journal.

First printing

All characters in this book are fictitious, and any resemblance to real persons, living or dead, is coincidental.

PublishAmerica has allowed this work to remain exactly as the author intended, verbatim, without editorial input.

ISBN: 1-60610-164-1
PUBLISHED BY PUBLISHAMERICA, LLLP
www.publishamerica.com
Baltimore

Printed in the United States of America

Contents

Introduction 7
"Am I Good Enough?" 9
Scars of Judgment 17
Airbrush 25
Eye Candy 30
It's All Relative 35
Snapshot 41
Skin Deep 48
Face-Off 56
Get Flawed 64
Get Real 72
Words from the Author 81

Introduction

    I know I'm not perfect, but can you embrace me? If I am not a dime piece, will you still accept me? If I never lose another pound, would you still keep looking at me? What if I stay 5'5, and weigh 155 pounds, could you still say that I am beautiful? I know that I'm not a zero, a four, or a six; but I am the size that fits you best. So why do I anger you? Is it something that I did? Do I walk the wrong way? Do I look too different? Am I not fitting in the way others say that I should? Am I the wrong shape, color, or size?

    I see you point out my imperfections one by one. You number them as if they are stains that you want and wish you could remove. When you stand on the scale, you look at me like I'm your worst enemy. You stare at those numbers and then you gaze back at me and say "fat bitch". You shake your head in disgust and you walk away enraged as if somehow I've let you down. I'm doing everything that I can to make you happy. When you see my reflection all you do is sigh. So tell me, how can I please you? How can I make you happy? What do I have to do for you to say that I'm good enough?

    I don't want to be your worst nightmare, but somehow I am. At night, you cry yourself to sleep because you think about how nasty, horrible, wrong, and disgusting I am. And when you get ready in the morning, you dress in the dark. You don't even look at me when you step out of the shower. Are you that displeased with me that you would deny me from a meal? Have I been that bad that you would cut me?

I've seen you go to the bathroom and I know what you do in there. I've seen you take those pills and laxatives and it hurts me every time you do. Like a slave, you push and press me to do things that I cannot do. You exercise day in and day out; and quite frankly, I'm exhausted. Over the years we've grown apart. Lately, you've been thinking about ending it all. I've listened to your comments about me. I've heard what your friends say. I was there when your boyfriend said that I was damaged goods. But why didn't you stand up for me? Why didn't you walk away? Instead, you got depressed and you rejected me.

I know that I'm not the best in your eyes, but I'm all you've got. Believe me when I say that I need you and you need me. I want you to love me. I want you to be proud of me. I want you to be excited when you see me. I want you to accept me. I hate seeing you hating to see me. I need to see you smile again, before you saw the billboards. I want things to go back to the way they were before you saw the magazines. I don't know how much more I can say. I want you to know that even though you've been ashamed of me, I've never been ashamed of you. I know that you don't love me, but maybe after you read this, somehow, you'll learn to.

Always and forever,
Your Body

"Am I Good Enough?"

Have you ever asked yourself that question? If you have, then you've asked the question that plagues every woman's mind. Chances are, you're fighting the very same battle that every woman has fought within herself. This happens to be the age-old question that has been the incurable curse upon many generations of women. It's the challenge that faces each and every one of us, whether young or young at heart. Despite our many achievements, it has been the one setback that continues to restrain and influence our lives. It has become the invisible wall that no one else can see or know that you're in.

Even though we all have lives to live, it is still the question that drives us to try harder and longer to prove that we are worthy, that we exist and that we are somebody. But at the same time there's a fear and desperation that's pushing our minds into overdrive as we battle self-esteem, relationships, careers, school, family; and the list goes on. And what's so angering about the whole thing is that we live day in and day out dealing with the same question. So to cope, we do greater things, we make more decisions, we add more to our schedules, we exercise an extra hour, we make more money, and we buy more things. But at the end of the day, life still hasn't brought the solution. It seems as if all the pleasures that once brought you joy and satisfaction now remind you of where you think you've fallen short.

How many times have these things led you to ask yourself if you were measuring up? How often have these issues caused you to dwell and meditate on whether or not you were doing enough or being a good enough person? If you're being truthful, it's happened more times than you can count. And for some of us, it's on a regular basis.

Whether you know it or not, these are the triggering questions that ignite a wildfire that easily consumes the true essence of which you are as a woman. This is the question that fuels an inferno of frustration, anger, anxiety, hopelessness, and a whirlwind of other things. Who would have thought or even imagined that these four words could cause you to lose focus and forget all the things that you used to love and enjoy about yourself and about life.

So let me ask you something. What if this plague can be healed? What if this battle can be won once and for all? What if this is the last time that you or I will ever have to face this challenge? What if you can finally overcome the one thing that's been overcoming you? I know you may think that what I'm asking you is impossible, but despite what you may think, it is absolutely possible.

Whether it be physically, relationally, emotionally, mentally, or any other area of your life; you don't have to live with lingering thoughts that cause you to look down on yourself. You don't have to put up with emotions that underestimate and beat down your potential and purpose. You can rise to the occasion and face head on the sole perpetrator and stalker of your heart, your mind, and your life. I wish that I could say that all you would have to do is dress a certain way, look a certain way, or achieve certain things, but I wouldn't be telling you the truth. All of these things are good and they give much satisfaction, but they aren't the solution. Not one of them has the ability to solve an issue that's rooted from the inside, out.

So let's cut to the chase and deal with it. Can you count the number of times that you have looked at your body in the mirror, and had a thought or image flash across your mind that made you feel inferior to some picture in a magazine? What about when you watched a show or viewed an advertisement that told you who you should be, what you have to have, or who you should look like, that it ended up making you think twice about your appearance and what you had to offer?

Well, if you're anything like the rest of us, not only did you think twice about what you saw, who you were, and what you had to offer, you also made some kind of effort to change it so that you could fit into the molded image before you. You made it your calling in life to be what it is that you see and hear about, so that you could fit in. If the results didn't match up with the image you saw, you felt guilty, ashamed, and unattractive — even to the point self-hate.

What you didn't know is that every time you questioned and pondered these things, you were going to war with self-doubt, which happens to be the issue that's rooted from the inside out. Now I know that self-doubt may seem harmless and irrelevant, but so does the wind — until it turns into a hurricane or tornado.

Believe it or not, self-doubt has the ability to do the exact same thing. It can turn into the storm of your life, by grabbing hold of your confidence, and causing you to go into a cycle of self-consciousness, self-abuse, self-deprecation, and self-destruction.

Self-doubt is the phantom to the opera of your life. It's the enemy to your inner-me. It attacks your identity and causes you to underestimate your own self-worth and value. Self-doubt is the reverse of self-acceptance, and it is the complete opposite of confidence. When you're not confident in whom you are as a person, an individual, and as a woman, you become shackled with the burdens of your own thoughts, feelings, and emotions. So instead of you believing in yourself and in your abilities, you're overshadowed with limitations and fears that hinder you from being and becoming all that you can be. You start forfeiting all the things that make you who you are. You stop fighting for what you believe in, and you start surrendering to the things that demean and diminish you from the inside out.

Self-doubt is the archenemy of your individuality and your uniqueness. It keeps you from making the most out of your life. It prevents you from living your life the way you deserve, which is in abundance, to the full, until it overflows. It's the little voice that whispers and tells you that you're nothing and that you can't make it. It says to you that you aren't qualified, and that you don't have what it takes. It tells you that you're fat, ugly, and that no body will ever want you. It says to you, that you don't need to break the mold and get outside of the lethal standards to actually become the woman that you were created and destined to be. It spawns fear and it limits you to only live where you "fit in".

When you're dealing with self-doubt, your answers and thoughts about who you are and how you look will never be the same. They will change when your emotions change, and vary based on your situation, your circumstance, or whatever season of life you happen to be in. It's kind of like a roller coaster ride; you go from one extreme to the next. If you do not conquer it, it can easily turn into the black hole of your life. Self-doubt changes the way you see yourself and how you think about yourself; and in extreme situations, it can even lead to suicide.

But all of that can be changed. The good news is that self-doubt isn't some mysterious mist, force, or storm that can't be reckoned with. In fact, here are some simple definitions for self-doubt: *Having a lack of confidence in who you are, or in your abilities, etc. Reproach or blame of yourself. Abuse of your health and well being. Having a second thought that is contrary or opposes who you know yourself to be. Representing you as having little or no value. Being excessively conscious of the way you look as an object of observation to others. Doubt turned inward. Or not believing in who you are, or what you can do.* Whichever you relate to the most, I want you to know that dealing with it doesn't have to be a war of the worlds. You don't have to bring out the heavy artillery in order to defeat it. All you have to do is reverse it. I know it may sound simple, but the truth is, is that you can overcome it. So let's do that.

Your first step to reverse self-doubt, which is the age-old question of "Am I good enough", is making positive declarations. However, making positive declarations doesn't mean that you focus on what you do not have. It doesn't mean that you just go around saying something nice or perky about yourself. It means that you start paying attention to what you do have. It means that you are taking the time out to reflect on who it is that you know yourself to be, and who it is that you desire to become.

If you were to take a good look at your thought life, you will see that self-doubt lingers and follows the "Am I's"; and so many of us are spending our lives being bombarded by the mess of it. Self-doubt is only a weed that chokes your faith and you cannot live victoriously when you are a victim to doubt. Why? Because, it takes faith to live this life; and I'm not talking about a religion. I'm talking about you having hope in the truth that says, no matter whom you are, where you've come from, or what you may be going through, you can overcome.

You can't let this get the best of you. There is so much more to you than what it is that you doubt. Sure, there are many influences, but you are the sole dictator and judge of the way you live your life. What you think about yourself has more of an affect, than what others think about you. Don't continue to doubt who you are. Don't continue to weigh and measure your self-worth on the scale of "Am I."

Instead, begin to turn it around and gain your self-confidence back by saying to yourself, "I Am". Make sure that you start believing it because who you are is very, very important. I know you may feel insignificant at times, but none of that will ever diminish your worth and value. You are worth living for, and your life is worth living. There is something that you bring and add to the earth that no one else can. Your life is mandatory. So put away any and all self-doubt that tries to tell you otherwise, because we need you despite what you may have heard or been told. You are important.

Do not ever again underestimate who you are and your self-worth by overestimating self-doubt. And if no one ever told you that you where good enough, or if you have ever wondered what, how, or why you're good enough, let me tell you what, how and why: Sweet heart, you are somebody. You are a unique structure. You have a purpose and you have a reason as to why you are here. As a matter of truth, you are here on purpose for a purpose. You are not a mistake. Your life is not an accident. You are fearfully (reverently) and wonderfully made. Whether you believe in God or not, you are here for destiny.

My love, we all have something special to do, and you are here because you have been destined for greatness. So don't let anybody tell you otherwise. Don't let anybody push you down. Don't let doubt or anyone stop you from doing what you dream. Don't let a thief steal your purpose in life. Hold on, and fight for what rightfully belongs to you. You deserve to live. You deserve to be loved. You deserve to be appreciated and not depreciated. You deserve to be celebrated and not tolerated; and I am here to tell you that you can come out. You can make it. Even though it may not happen overnight, it is a process that you will complete. After all, you and I are a work in progress. So the next time you begin to doubt yourself, immediately begin to confess the opposite. Stop selling yourself short. You've done too much and come too far to cut away all the things that add so much to your essence and splendor. It's important for you to remember that who you are is not based on any emotion, situation, relationship, or circumstance. You are who you are because you're the only one of you; and that's significant.

Make it your battle cry for victory to get rid of the "Am I's" and start saying "I Am". It's time for you to reverse self-doubt. Therefore, I don't ever want you to ask yourself again "Am I good enough?" I want you to now say to yourself "I Am Good Enough!"

Scars of Judgment

Everyone has something that has scared them. We all have a place somewhere deep within, where we bear the marks that remind us of a time and place where the unthinkable has been said or happened. All of us at some point and time have lived the reality of the thing we feared most. I'm quite sure that you can remember the exact moment that depressed, changed, and destroyed your innocence and your identity. And it was in those times when we were first introduced to pain. It was at that very moment when we were left exposed and alone to be victimized by inward anger and outward judgments that were triggered by what someone else said, did, or implied.

You know what that feels like right? You know what it's like when you have someone point out all of the things about you that don't fit, are irregular, too large, too small, undone, under developed, and not good enough. It's almost as if they've taken a survey of your body and marked all of the places that they think need improvement, or need to be brought to your attention, said something out loud about it, and then posted them for the whole world to see and before you know it, what one person started ten more are continuing, which in turn has started a whole snowball effect of criticism toward you and your body.

As if you weren't already having thoughts about who you are and how you look, there are now eleven other people who agree that your breasts are too small, your nose is too big, your thighs are too thick, your feet too big, your arms too long, your eyes too slanted, your complexion is flawed, you're not the right shape, your butt is flat; and in general, there is nothing right and beautiful about you. Now everyone is saying openly and shouting from the roof tops what you've already been telling yourself secretly for quite sometime.

The secrets out and it's exposed; and so are you. Now everyone knows what you've been hiding under the makeup, the jewelry, the clothes, the shoes, shopping, food, all of the exercise, the drinking, the drugs, the parties, relationships, fights, and the list goes on. Yet they do nothing about it. They don't stop because you're hurting or because you're backed into a corner. They don't let up at all because you shed a tear. They use it as another weapon of mass destruction toward your defeat and demise.

Having everyone know your secret is the nightmare on Elm Street. It's the dream of standing naked before friends, foes, and strangers, as they laugh and scoff at every detail, but instead of you waking up, you're already awake and unable to escape the relic. Even now, I know that you can think of things that have been said to you, done to you, and spoken about you that have really impacted how you see yourself, others, and life.

Now days it's hard to deal with those outside influences that affect, infect, and reflect how you see yourself, and how you approach everyday life. As if the feelings of insignificance aren't already prevalent and bold within your own heart and mind, now you have to put up with the mess that's bombarding you everywhere you go. It's almost like you can't catch a break. Just when you get a handle on one thing, something else has come in its place to drive you completely chaotic. Today it's about your body and tomorrow, some stupid conversation about how you look, which is still about your body; and all of a sudden, the grass isn't greener on the other side, because there's crap everywhere you go.

So how are you supposed to deal with that? How are you supposed to get a handle and confront the very labels that have changed your life, your perception, your expectations, and your confidence as a young lady and as woman? What are you supposed to do when there's always some kind of bar or standard that's raised every single day that you have to reach before the day is done, but before you know it, you're hanging on trying not to let go because in an instant, things have already changed right before your eyes.

Well, you take another step and you start building up your self-esteem. It's so easy for the perfect image to become an endless charade of who is and who isn't what is and what isn't. For so many of us, we've never really had the chance to even have any self-esteem — let alone the tools to build any. It seems as if these things have been going on for so long, that even the thought of having any esteem is on the endangered list, and on the verge of extinction; and for some of you, it already is. The good news is that self-esteem isn't something that you lose and can never find again. It's more like a spring. You can suppress it and make it shrink, but once you take away all the pressures and forces that are holding it down, it springs back like a pop-tart out of a toaster.

I know how easy it is to believe that what someone else has to say about you must be true, because you think that they have the better view, but that couldn't be further from the truth. The truth of the matter is, is that the best view is the one that you have through your own eyes. No one can tell you that what you have is good or bad. They can't even say that who you are, is or isn't good enough. Only you can determine that.

Whatever the case may be, don't let it continue to weigh heavily upon your heart. I want you to realize that all they have is an opinion and chances are that their opinion is a belief and judgment that solely rests on grounds that are insufficient in producing certainty. All they have is a personal view and attitude that's aimed at you to cover up their own insecurities and dislikes about who they are. It's a judgment that falls short of truth and reality.

Therefore, I only have one thing to say to you. So listen carefully to these three words: "DON'T BELIEVE IT!" Don't you go and give them dominion over your mind, your will, your body, or your emotions. Don't allow them to gain access to your identity. I'm not telling you that these things never happened, but I am saying that they never should have happened. You are the only one of you, so stop believing everything that you hear. Make a stand, because if you don't stand for something, you will fall for anything. You need to find out what it is that you believe about yourself based on what you know about you, and not on someone else's philosophy or fantasy.

It's about time you get a good grip on your own life and stop letting vain imaginations pull on the reins of your heart, only to steer you in a direction that you aren't willing to go and can't get out of. You need to determine the genuine from the counterfeit, the reality from the fiction. Once you do, no one else will be able to define you or place you into a category that is the opposite of who you already know yourself to be. You won't ever again fall victim to judgments that leave scars to constantly remind you of what "they" said.

You have to learn and understand that one of the most potent and deadly things that we do as women, is letting someone else put a price and value on what is priceless and one of a kind. In case you don't know what I'm talking about, let me tell you: its YOU — spirit, soul, and body. It's all of you no matter your age, creed, race, culture, ethnicity, size, or weight. Every part of you is beyond any amount of money or possessions. What you have and who you are is a gift that will keep on giving, even long after you've gone. It's called a legacy and a heritage. It's what you have that no one else does. It's what you create that no one else has even thought of. So open up your eyes and see that what you're looking for, you already have.

Regardless to whether society agrees with you or not, you need to know that you've got what it takes and it's because you have what it takes that you're all that and a bag of chips, with a sundae on the side. You have it all hidden and buried within. So grab a shovel a pail, and a flashlight, and go find yourself. Go and see who it is that you truly are. Uncover and unfold the manifold splendor, beauty, and essence of you.

You may have thought that I would be talking to you about all your bruises and wounds, but if you were to be honest, you've already done enough of that to last you into eternity. I know and you know what the title of this chapter says, but if you were to take another look at it you would see that the one thing about a scar is that it's past. Yes, the memory and impression is still present and maybe even the emotions of it, but the truth of the matter is, is that it's time for you to finally heal and move on.

I know that it's still fresh as if it was yesterday when all that came knocking at your door — and for some of you that just may be the case, but this entire chapter is written for you to put the aloe on, rub the cocoa butter in, and begin to take the next step to move forward. It may sting a bit in your heart, but you have got to leave it behind and get your mind renewed. You need to learn how to exercise the positive realms of your life. Take a spiritual, emotional, mental, and physical shower, and wash away all of those grievances that have kept you shackled and tormented. Everything in you can ache, but once you get your release you'll see that being refreshed, restored, and free is far greater than anything in the world.

It may be hard work now, but in the end you'll understand that it was worth the labor. Let go of negative relationships. Throw away all the old things that remind you of that day, season, and moment in your life. There's no point in you keeping that poison in, with, or around you. I want you to strive for your freedom. Begin to hunger and thirst for the release of your purpose and destiny as a virtuous woman.

You wouldn't swim in sewage or bathe in bleach would you? So stop drowning yourself in the past. Reject the lies that you have been told. You need to know that any lie whether big or small can never turn into the truth. It may have been presented in a persuasive way to make you believe that what was said or done was true, but it was and still is a lie. It was like a wolf in sheep's clothing. You are not damaged goods. You're not a mistake. You are not unworthy. You are not ugly. You're not a misfit, and you are not unlovable.

If you can recall any demeaning word or thing that anyone has ever spoken about you or done to you, I want you to make it up in your mind right now to forget about it. Make it up in your heart to believe that none of those things make you who you are. Know within yourself that it doesn't define you. I want you to know that you are a woman to be cherished, valued, and highly esteemed—first by you, and then by others. You need to command it first from yourself so that you can then expect it from others.

Do not tolerate any longer anyone who "spits" on who you are whether it be in body, personality, character, intelligence, etc. expect more of and from yourself, but not to the degree of abuse or self-destruction; but of esteem and honor. I cannot tell you enough how wonderfully beautiful you are. You have more than you realize.

Even though it's easy for others to put shame and blame on someone else for their own downfalls and shortcomings, that's no excuse for anyone to hurt you, or you to turn around and hurt yourself. You are not to blame for someone else's choices. You are not to be punished for another person's consequences. You did not bring any of this upon yourself. You do not deserve to be hurt in any way. It is not acceptable, so don't tolerate it. You're worth so much more and you deserve much more.

You know who you are, and you know that what I'm saying is true. So if you don't know what else to do, make like a tree and leave. Make like a banana and split. And in movie terms, "Run Forest run!" Get away from all the things that are killing you slowly from the inside out. Why? Because there's hope for you. There is more to your life than what you can see. You have a future. There is hope on the other side of that mountain. So let's climb it and come on through to the other side. So let's take this step together. Let's begin to build your self-esteem. It's time for you to gain a favorable expression of respect for yourself. After all, you're worth it.

Airbrush

It used to be that when you took a picture, what you see is what you get. Now, before you even develop or print a picture out, you can take away anything that you don't like. You can edit somebody or something in or out of the picture in order to make it look exactly how you think that it should. You can cut away and shade anything that you don't like and replace it with something more satisfying. It's like having your own way of presenting a first impression of who you imagine yourself to be. You no longer have to show any blemishes. Instead, all you have to do is airbrush it, and instantly, you've erased all imperfections. Thanks to digital, you can now have the perfect picture.

Everywhere you look, there is someone or something that has been touched by a virtual brush to shade and take away irregular fits in order to make it look good and have appeal. You no longer have to suck in, tuck away, or gird them, because today's technology is so great in doing all of that for you with the click of a button. However, there is one thing that I've discovered about airbrushing that surprised me. "It isn't real." All of it is temporary. No matter what you do or how you do it, there is nothing permanent to an airbrush. All it does is cover up what it is that you don't want exposed.

It's the master manipulator and the ultimate phenomenon. It's the magician's illusion—with you being both the magician and the illusion. But hey, it's a win/win situation right? Wrong. There is only one way to describe airbrushing, and that's with the word: ARTIFICIAL. As wonderful and helpful as it is, it's still something that's made by human skill to be fanciful, illusory, and delusory in nature. It's the coded message to all women that says who you are would be much better if you touch it up a little bit. There isn't one woman on the face of this planet, who hasn't thought to herself "If I could only".

If you've ever had that moment were you've taken a picture and experienced that feeling of shock and disgust about what you saw in the photo, then you know what I'm talking about. Do you remember asking yourself "Is that really what I look like?" followed by "I can't believe my (fill in the blank) looks like that?" If you're anything like the rest of us, you've also said to yourself, "Delete"; and you know that what I'm saying in true. After all, we've all been there. We've all done this.

Which leads me to ask you this: If you could take a picture of yourself, what would you airbrush? If you could cut away and shade what you hate the most about you, what would it be? If you could, right now, take an eraser and a pencil and remove anything, what would you draw in its place? How would you sketch your body? What would be the perfect you? Whose nose would you have? Whose eyes would you draw? Whose hair would you shade in? Whose figure would you outline?

I'm sure that you have someone in mind that you would love to trade bodies with. Without even second-guessing yourself, you probably know two or three, or maybe even more things about you that you would swap at the drop of a dime. With today's products and opportunities, you can actually come closer to achieving it. There are creams, surgeries, workouts, treatments, diets, self-helps, videos, and talk shows; step by step guides, books, magazines, articles, experts, and the list only increase via the Internet.

Everybody's got something that they swear by; and some have the actual proof of its success. Yet, despite all of these things, so many women and young girls are falling by droves into eating disorders, addictions, and many other things to try and attain the airbrush — the image of perfection. Our daughters are dying and suffering silently so that they can be the best, look the best, and become what they are seeing displayed before them every day of their lives.

Airbrushing has built such an exaggerated ostentation, that it's easier and more instinctual to believe something that has superficial characteristics, rather than natural compositions. In other words, fake is embraced and deemed more acceptable than being unique, distinct, and diverse. We're continuously putting pressures and expectations on ourselves that's diminishing us very slowly; and I don't know about you, but enough is enough.

We need to take a long look at what's happening, so that we can come out of this. As women, we need take another step and start decoding unrealistic expectations. It's imperative to know the difference between realistic and unrealistic possibilities. Even though it's okay to have goals, desires, and expectations for yourself and the way you look, they shouldn't jeopardize your life or your well being.

Regardless to the many appealing distractions, I don't want you to get caught up in the maze of do I or don't I. For so many of us, it's much easier to accept other people than it is to accept ourselves. But why is that? Could it be because we think that nothing could possibly be wrong with them? Or how about the thought and assumption that their lives have to be better than ours? Or is it simply because it's easier to reject them if they fail, than it would to be to reject ourselves?

Whatever the case, there's one thing that you should know: "Things aren't always, as they seem." You may wish and dream about having what someone else possesses, but the truth of the matter, is that it you'll be cheating yourself. No matter what you do, what they have will always belong to them. You can have every kind of nip tuck to look like their identical twin, but you will still be you—just with a counterfeit reflection.

They are one of a kind and so are you. You will never have their fingerprint, and they will never have yours. You may think that you share similar likes, and dislikes, but no matter what, you're still the only one of you; and that's a good thing. I know you may not see it right now, but you're a good picture. I know that there are times when you may not be able to tell, but you possess a radiance that shines in every photo you take. Woman to woman, I want you to know that you don't have to airbrush who you are to make yourself "more". Your presence in itself is already more than enough.

So the next time you encounter anything that has been "made

up", remind yourself that it's artificial. No matter how good it looks, it's the magic of airbrushing that's presenting the illusion of a perfect picture.

Eye Candy

Looks can be very compelling, especially when they are the demands of culture. Everywhere you look, there is someone or something looking back at you to reflect who it is, and what it is that you are to do, wear, think, and become. In a generation where fashion lies on every mind, every address, every page, every billboard and every corner, there isn't a single woman who hasn't been influenced by the bold images of beauty, and sexuality. Regardless to the amounts of money we spend each season to keep in style, somehow, the race for woman of the year is never given to the same woman twice. When it comes down to the way a woman looks, there is no happy medium. The "to do" list only gets longer by the day, as we each check off what works and what doesn't. It seems as if there's never enough time, money, or product that can keep us in the game so that we can actually finish and win. Now day's you're either in or you're out. You fit or you don't. You eat or you diet. You succeed or you fail. There are always words being spoken to make us feel like hell. We no longer possess the luxury of being proud of who we are and the gift that we have been given. Many of us don't even stand a chance to "be", because we're constantly being reminded that who we are it isn't enough.

Now, it doesn't take a genius to know that the rules of the

BODY IMAGE

game have changed. There are now penalties, where there used to be leniency. It seems like every time we turn around we're striking out at something, or we're getting called out on our setbacks. Even the way the game is being played seems like it has been fixed; and that's turning costly. Not so much in finance, but in the fullness and fairness of the way we live, move, and have our being.

As women, our quality of life is being depreciated because of our drive to keep up with and beat "the girl next door." What used to be a friendly and edifying competition has turned into a blood sport. We no longer give genuine compliments from one woman to another. Instead, we criticize and critique every inch of each other, from head to toe. We examine in detail what it is that she has that we don't, or what it is that we have that she doesn't. We survey one another's conduct, presentations, and associations to make certain that what we have is still on point. The majority of us have even gone to the extremes of taking mental tallies and notes about where we are in comparison to where she is, just so that we can remain confident that we're good enough.

So let's face the facts. There is a serious breach among us women today, when we feel threatened by another woman. There's something missing when we don't want another female looking better than us. I know you know what it's like to get angry because you see another chick getting all of the attention. It's as if there's something about her that rubs you the wrong way; and we've all been there. Especially when jealousy, chaos, and all hell is about to brake loose, because of some girl who came into the room with an agenda. It's as if there's some kind of Jekyll and Hyde gene that makes us turn into a she-devil when we see another woman who has the "it" factor.

So how do you get back your quality of life? How do you mend the breach? How can you stay to finish and win the game without it first finishing you? Is there a place where can you find a happy medium? Can you handle the demands of culture, and still possess the fullness in which you are — even when the game isn't fair? The answer for these questions is simple, but it involves your willingness to make another step and start recognizing unhealthy comparisons.

There is a very fine line between friendly fire, and assassination. Therefore, you have to realize that every time you compare yourself to another woman, you're taking a fatal shot and depreciating your own worth and value. Even though there is nothing wrong with looking to see what she looks like, you have to get a grip on why you're looking, and how often you look. Just because you see another woman who looks good, doesn't disqualify you from looking good also. As long as you keep your focus and attention on the other woman, you are robbing yourself and others of a wonderful opportunity to know, enjoy, and embrace who you are.

There is no sense in you driving yourself insane because you're constantly wondering and fearing that the girl next door is better off than you are. You will never be able to enjoy your life and all the things that you have to offer as long as you continue to look over your shoulder, across the street, or around the corner. Your life is supposed to be fun. You're supposed to enjoy it with your girlfriends, but when you get upset because she has what you wish you had, or vice versa, things will go down hill very quickly. Before you know it, you've reached the point of complete and absolute rivalry; which is what unhealthy comparisons are.

Whether you believe me or not, it is possible for you to live the life that you dream, as long as what you're dreaming isn't in comparison to, and doesn't already belong to someone else. The whole purpose of a dream is to get a picture of who you are, and live that out in your own destiny. You have been given a gift that no one can take away. It's one of rarity, and significance; and you possess it. The gift that you have is full of life and splendor that exceeds all boundaries and limitations. And if you don't know what this gift is, let me tell you: "It's being a woman. It's having the ability to do great things, by living life so that you may in return, give life."

So don't continue to make unhealthy comparisons of yourself to a billboard, an advertisement, a sibling, a friend, a stranger, or even to the words that someone speaks to you or about you. It doesn't matter how the game is being played. You can still win in this life, and actually finish on top. You can handle anything culture demands from you, if you know and believe that who you are is not found in what you do or how you do it. Who you are is found in who you will become and you have a right to be yourself without loosing your life.

You can rediscover the quality of your life when you stop going out and overestimating what you see. Chances are that what you see isn't all that it's cracked up to be. Why? Because looks by themselves, can be very deceiving. There are many good eye candies out there, but very few of them are a real and good treat. So whether you think that you have the "it" factor or not, it is still your responsibility to make sure that your personality and your character isn't distasteful; and that's the happy medium. When you spend more time taking an inside look at yourself, you'll find out that you won't have the time or the desire to pay so much attention to someone else.

I want you to see how imperative it is for you to get a revelation about your life. It is so vital for you to grasp the truth about you, so that you can really start living the fullness of what your life has to offer. This is why it is needful for you to mend the breach by knowing that there can be more than one woman of the year. It isn't limited to any particular award, classification, standard, opinion or person and it shows no favoritism. All you have to do is switch the letter 'a' with the letter 'e', and you will see that all women can be a woman of the year. The good news about that is that YOU are one of them.

It's All Relative

There are three numbers that rule every woman's life. Numbers that somehow dictate who you are what you're worth, and where you're headed. They linger like a fog to cloud the vision of every woman who stands before them. They are more than a reflection, because these numbers never lie. It's almost like a haunting—one that visits you everyday, and every night. They follow you like a shadow, constantly reminding you that they're there and no matter where you go or what you do, their whispers are there to tell you over and over again the lullaby of "Humpty Dumpty".

Every time you take a stand before their council, these three numbers are the unforgiving and merciless judges ruling and raining down their verdict; sentencing you to D.E.A.T.H. (Disappointment, Exasperation, Anxiety, Turmoil, and Hate). They possess the power to take captive or set free any and all, who come into their domain. All of their counsel is one of defeat and hopelessness, and even when there is good news, they will immediately let you know that you could do better. There is never a congratulations or a celebration of how far you've come. It's only the numbing replies of "so close, but yet so far".

Now I'm quite sure that you know by now what I'm talking about, but if you don't, I'll enlighten you. These three judges are the numbers on the scale. The ones that consume everything and determine all that we do. I'm talking about the infamous three. The ones in which our entire lives revolve around. They tell us what we should eat, the way we should dress, what we talk about, what articles we read in a magazine, and the way we present ourselves, our confidence, etc.

The numbers on the scale are the reason why we diet. They're our excuse to treat ourselves like rags for six weeks. They are the purpose for why we take our bodies, our emotions, and our minds through such strenuous cycles of highs and lows, ins and outs, treats and denials. Week after week, month after month, year after year, we go through the endless process of trying to bum away yesterday's 'cheat'. What would otherwise be another ordinary trip to the grocery store, has now turned into the forbidden journey of the week because of the temptation to walk down the cookie isle.

We now count the calories in a bowl of fruit, instead of just simply biting into an apple. When a menu at a restaurant is placed before us, we look for the least appetizing dish, or the lightest entree to make sure that we don't "over indulge". Then we have the nerve to only take a few bites out of that tasteless meal, and skip desert, only to return home just as hungry as when we left. By the end of the night, we can't even rest, because our stomachs are howling and we continue to smell the forbidden aroma of the fried chicken that our friend had that we wished we had ordered. And once we're asleep, we only awake the next day to do it all over again.

Whether you believe this it or not, a diet isn't supposed to be a death sentence, or life without parole. It was never meant to be a means of boot camp or torture for you or your body, but somehow it has surely turned into one. Now day's it's boldly taught to all women that it's normal to not eat, and to count the calories of what you do. It's in every other commercial and it has become the obsession and the hot topic of conversation among the girls.

In an alarming way, these numbers have evolved into a 24-hour cell with no bars, no windows, no doors, no keys, and no way out. It's almost like the more you use them, the more they abuse you. We submit and endure the pressures and pain of these numbers every single day, like they are the landlords of our minds and the pimps of our bodies. And if you don't believe me, take a look at the statistics: 1,000 women die each year in America from anorexia. Four out of five women say that they hate their bodies. 90 percent of fashion models say that they have low self-esteem. So what does that tell you? It tells me that the numbers on the scale have become our drugs of choice. We've gotten addicted to the high of what we see and don't see. And before we knew what was going down, it was too late. We were already engulfed within the potency of its product.

So I have to ask you: Does what you see truly reflect who you are? Have the numbers on the scale become the rulers in which you measure and weigh your self worth and value? Have you been walking the fine line between Bulimia and Anorexia? Are you the girl who will do whatever it takes to achieve the single size and be the "perfect" weight?

If you are, then I have something to tell you. If you have

stretched your limits or experimented with certain diets or other things to help you lose weight, you have ignited a fuse on the inside of you that in the end, will eventually cost you more than you are willing to pay; and that's not the right way for you to go. I know that it may seem like your only choice, but the truth of the matter is that it isn't. You have so much more to live for, than you do to die for. There is more to your life than what you see come up in weights and measurements. This is why it's time for you to take yet another step and defuse self-torment.

Self-torment is a weapon of mass destruction. It is a ticking bomb on the inside of you, and it's only a matter of time before it goes off. When it does, it won't explode, it will implode; and that's not an exaggeration. However, the devastation isn't in the impact of the implosion. It's in the ripple affect. Each and every time you go to the extremes to move the numbers on the scale; you're the one who's truly suffering. You're putting your body through the kind of exhaustion that it was never destined or designed to experience. Instead of your body keeping up and maintaining life, it's withering away. It's going into survival mode in order to keep up with your demands.

Too often, no one else knows that you're being abused and victimized by your own self-will; and you're not alone in this thing. You'd be shocked to see how many other women are going through what you are experiencing right now. I've been there when the end result was the exact same number as it was six months ago. I know what it's like to think to yourself over and over again how you could eradicate these numbers. I understand how relentless it is to live through the metal beat downs and feelings of failure, because what you thought and hoped to see, didn't appear. I know what it means to give the infamous three, power and reign over your mind, your will, your emotions, your life, and your body: But I have good news. YOU'VE GOT THE POWER! You have the power over the scale and the three numbers that rule it. You have the power to determine what it is that you see before and after you step onto it. And no matter how you may feel before, during, and after the entire process, you have got the power to choose whether or not you're going to let any of it get the best of you. Even when you continue to get the same results week after week and month after month, you've still got the power to take charge over the thoughts that are running through your mind telling you that you're a failure, and that you will never change.

You have the power and the ability to overcome every doubt, fear, irritation, and image that you have starring you down everyday. So I want to encourage you to stop trying to please the scale, because it won't happen. No matter what you do, it will always tell you the complete opposite of what you are yearning to hear. As long as you continue weigh your life and who you are on what it is that you see come up in the display column, you will never win with the numbers on the scale. Even when they are be very convincing, the truth of the matter is that these numbers are no more or no less than digits. You're not going to get any more out of them as you would a rock. They are what they are, and all that's all they will ever be. So get rid of the self-torment. Because your worth and value goes far beyond whatever numbers you see.

Now I know that what I'm saying may sound crazy to you right now, but I'm telling you exactly what you need to hear. Because when it all boils down to it, your life is dependent upon these words. So if you don't hear anything else that I have to say, please remember this one thing: YOU are worth living for! There isn't enough money, attention, compliments, or celebrity in this world that can even come close to the priceless wonders that is YOUR LIFE. So I urge you to make the decision to CHOOSE LIFE. Make it up in your mind that you will defuse self-torment so that you can live and not die.

Hell is real, but it doesn't have to be your reality. You don't have to sacrifice who you are or your body in order to become what you see displayed before you. Why? Because life is more than numerals. It's more than counting or loosing inches and pounds, and it's in that reason that I know and am confident that there is HOPE for you. You have nothing to be ashamed of or afraid of. It's not too late for you. As long as you have breath in your body, you can come out of this with your life. With the right help, counsel, and support, you can beat this. You can win.

Snapshot

People have a way of making you feel uncomfortable in your own skin. They know how to point out and bring to your attention what you don't have, what you need to have, what you should hide, what you need to stay away from, and what you should hate about yourself. It's impressive and shocking to see how they have mastered the art of divide and conqueror by making you trust, believe, and rely on their rules, their expectations, and their guidelines as to how your life should be. It's almost as if they have made it their theme and goal in life to survey, study, and test who you are, with the sole purpose of bringing out the worst in you.

Now you believe that you are too short and too fat. You now imagine yourself being a slender size zero or one, instead of a healthy four, eight, or ten. You believe that extreme dieting and exercise are supposed to be the goal and focus of everyday life. You are completely dedicated to the demands of being fit. It's all that you think about. You're constantly spending your days trying to figure out ways to obtain this dream, so that you can finally be satisfied with being who it is that everyone else is dying to become.

You now have multiple places on your body that you are obsessed with, which beforehand were completely unbeknownst to you. There are images and concepts tattooed in the center of your mind that are constantly bringing to your attention the places where you have fallen short. You have harassing thoughts and ideas swirling around in your head telling you that there is something about you that could use a little improvement. All day long, these thoughts are telling you that it's okay to push yourself a little further. After all, if there's no pain, then there's no gain.

So in order to keep up appearances, you make the necessary changes, improvements, and subtractions that will make you fit into the sequence and flow of culture. You make sure that what they see is what will be accepted and not rejected. For the time being, all of it is exciting because you're getting the feed back and the attention that you want and worked so hard to get, but what you didn't know was that the end result of all of this would be the permanent impressions that you are left with physically, mentally, and emotionally.

You didn't prepare for the loss and damages that have completely ravaged and changed the way you view yourself. You didn't anticipate the consequences of what you now believe about who you are. Somehow you were blinded from the predicted war that would eventually occur in your heart and mind at the end of the day, when you would come face to face with the dissatisfaction of the way you look. Now you have questions that you can't find an answer to. You have struggles that no one seems to care that you are experiencing and to top it all off, you have constant reminders of everything that has gone down.

So what are you supposed to do when what you see is all that you meditate on? What do you do when the snap shot of who you are, is less than who you want to be? How are you supposed to change what you believe about yourself, when it's all that you can think about? Well, you eventually have to make another step and begin to refocus your self-perception.

Self-perception is defined as the way a person becomes aware of, knows, and identifies who they are by way of their senses. It is their apprehension of the way they envision, understand, and project themselves to be. In simpler terms, self-perception is the way you see yourself, which makes it the most powerful tool in your life. You can use it to either build yourself up, or tear yourself down.

Self-perception is the most common means by which we make our judgments, conclusions, and calculations of how much we are worth, and whether or not we have what it takes to be someone important and influential in life. Self-perception is also a means in which we establish the roles that we will play and live out. It is a self-fulfilling prophecy that determines what we will expect to receive from others, from ourselves, and from life in general. This is the very reason why so many women and young girls do not like who they are or what they see. It's why they have given up their freedom to choose, so that they can live their lives in the shadows of "the next craze".

The self-perception that you have right now can be traced back to a day and time where someone said or did something that molded and framed the way you perceive yourself. So the things that you see with your eyes and hear with your ears will eventually become your projection and understanding of who you envision, believe, and know yourself to be. This can become a major problem if you are downloading the wrong things. In fact, what and how you see is linked to the words that you have heard which in turn scanned itself into your thought life. What takes place in your thoughts has a direct connection to whom or what you have been listening to. And that simply means that what you allow to have access to into your eyes and your ears, will ultimately become the download of your thoughts, and will manifest your self-perception.

Now as silly as all of that may have sounded, it is absolutely true. If you were to start paying closer attention to what and you are listening to and occupying your time with, you are guaranteed to uncover the source of your own self-perception. You are most likely to unfold the very root and source of why you hate parts of your body. You will reveal the true reason why you think so low and badly about yourself. Without any doubt, you will receive a revelation of who you really are.

I know how easy it is to perceive other people better than we perceive ourselves. It's almost like we think that what they have is somehow better than what we have. It's in those times when we are the most likely to depreciate who we are, by how we see. It's not hard to compare and contrast what another person has verses what you have. It's all how you look at it. There is no one size fits all. You have to do what fits you best.

For example, when there are people and things around you that are constantly put you down, or telling you to make some kind of alteration to feel better, eventually you will start to

BODY IMAGE

believe that what they are saying is true. The moment you begin to believe in what it is that they are saying, you have just subtracted and divided the most essential thing that distinguishably gives you the ability to see, know, and identify who you are, which is what your self-perception is.

So woman to woman, I challenge you to find out who or what you're investing your time in. Take the time out to uncover the words that you are hearing, believing, and telling yourself. Then to count up the cost and if the sum total of what you believe and perceive isn't worth what you are willing to pay or sacrifice, then you need to let it go. As hard as that may sound to do, you really need to carefully weigh it in proper perspective, and ask yourself if it's worth it. You need to ask yourself if these standards, rules, and expectations that you have for yourself are worth the destruction and misery of your life.

You have to determine whether or not such pain is worth your health, hope, and happiness. (And in case you may be thinking this, pain **does not** equal gain. Pain is pain, and it doesn't add anything to your life—unless you're giving birth. And I'm quite sure that you aren't, seeing that you would be reading this book.) After you have weighed that in your own heart and mind, then you make a decision. Hopefully it will be one that is based from within, and not from without.

Therefore, I want you to take a good look at yourself, and write down all of the words that come to your mind about you. Afterwards, I want you to go through each and every one of those words and take an honest view of the snap shot. Chances are that none of those words originated from you. More often than naught, the words that you have written have come from outside sources that you have allowed to hack into the mainframe of your heart and mind. As you search those inward depths, you will unfold the truth. Eventually, you will come across the good news that says, "If you have the wrong self-perception, you can change it by changing what it is that you hear and see."

You can change what you believe and perceive about yourself. You can change what it is that you say about yourself in your heart. Since you only have 24 hours in a day, you should do everything in your might to spend that time wisely. So don't continue to waste your time with things or people who don't edify you. Why? Because people and things can only do one of four things in your life: They will add, subtract, multiply, or divide. Believe me when I say that you don't want, nor do you need to have a life that's filled with division and subtraction.

I want you to see yourself in a manner that is uplifting and elegant. Do not allow yourself any longer to have a self-perception that is degrading and demeaning. You are fearfully and wonderfully made. There is no one else who has the beauty and radiance that you possess. It doesn't matter what someone else says about you. What matters, is what you believe about yourself. That's what self-perception is. It's how you see who you are and if what you see is pleasing in your own eyes, then it really doesn't matter what anyone else has to say about you — be it positive or negative.

So the next time you take a look at yourself in any way, remember that what you see is absolutely wonderful.

Regardless to how you may feel in that moment, you have to refocus your self-perception, and speak those things that are encouraging and motivating. Even when you read things in a magazine or see an advertisement that may tempt you to second guess yourself, shake all that off, and set your heart and mind on that which is going to build and uplift you. Keep your focus on what you have to offer, not on what you don't. Why? Because what you have to offer, is far more beneficial, profitable, and meaningful than what you don't. What you have to offer will be a blessing and a contribution, not only to your life, purpose, and destiny, but also to the lives of all of those who you will touch and help in one way or another.

Allow your positive self-perception to help you embrace the wonders of who you are. If no one else will tell you that you are worth it, tell yourself and if you still need someone to tell you, then I will. Honey, YOU ARE WORTH IT! So I encourage you to keep going. Continue to raise your standards of how you see yourself. Don't stop when it gets hard—and it will get hard. Instead, make every effort to raise your head high and be the unique woman that you were created and purposed to be. You have what it takes, and you will make it all the way. How do I know? I know, because I believe in you.

Skin Deep

Zero used to mean nothing. Now it's the ultimate goal in a young girl and woman's life. There are so many tips out there to help you come that much closer to reaching perfection, that there are very few of us who haven't already reached our hand into the cookie jar to taste and see what this procedure is like, or how this regiment works. There are so many of us, who have already taken the bait, that hardly anyone has actually stopped to think where this is going to end up. Without even knowing it, some of us are headed toward an unfortunate collision with reality, because we've neglected to count up the cost of pursuing perfection.

There are so many women and young girls today, who don't truly understand that they are playing rush and roulette with their lives. They don't take the time to evaluate and reevaluate the consequences of their choices and actions. Each and every time they make the decision to alter who they are without properly identifying why they're making such a minor or extreme modification, they are playing a dangerous game with their life and it's only a matter of time before they make a costly and maybe even a deadly mistake.

It's amazing to see some of the extreme's that we go through as women to be the perfect fit. Whether its botox, plastic surgery,

BODY IMAGE

cosmetics, weigh watchers, tea diets, cleansing, laxatives, pills, makeovers, makeup, fashion, hair coloring, and the lists are limitless. In our own hearts and minds, we want desperately to present a silhouette that we're happy to show everybody — even if everybody is only ourselves. We are all looking for the right thing that will finally complete the ensemble and make us who it is that we've been wishing, dreaming, and desiring to be; and we've all been there.

All of us have made at some point and time, the ultimate wish of the heart to look like this and have all of that. We've all been at that place where we want to look young and livelong. It's like we're trying to become the "It" girl. You know the one who has the right shape, the right size, the right look, the right walk, the right attraction, the right age, the right image, the right inches, the right voice, the right accessory, and the right Bo. We do whatever is necessary to create and become her. Whether it's cutting, breaking, gluing, stitching, tucking, shading, lining, or injecting.

We are dying to be perfect, because we have the idea that anything less than perfection isn't good enough. We have discontentment within ourselves because we believe that who we are lies in how well we can live up to a standard of acceptance and flawlessness. We even have these voices in our heads that push us try harder to obtain that ideal reflection. They come to us daily and say that we have to try this, and we have to do that in order to be just right. And if we don't, then we're worthless and unattractive because we're missing out on something great.

So to keep the voices down, we take the pills. We schedule the appointments, we make the shakes, we buy the formulas, we use the foundations, and we study the commercials and advertisements, but what we didn't consider was that some of these makeovers, transformations, and alterations are irreversible. Not so much in the physical nature, but in our emotions as well. We didn't stop and think about the permanent decisions that would drastically change our lives, and how we wouldn't be able to click our heels and return ourselves back to how it used to be. But what's so devastating about all of this it is that often times, we didn't know or appreciate what it was that we had, until it was too late.

So I have to ask you: What price are you paying for your looks? How much has this already cost you? How far are you planning to venture in order to obtain the perfect image? There is so much focus on the outer woman, that we've all become superficial in one way or another. Regardless to who you are you have made some kind of adjustments to blend into the arena of life, celebrity, culture, and entertainment; and there's nothing wrong with that. The problem comes when you lose your balance and fall into the rabbit hole of having to have it all — despite the ripple effect that it may have on you, your body, your emotions, your thoughts, your feelings, your mindset, or anyone who is close to you.

In this day and time it's so easy for you to do that. There are 8,000 images that go through your eyes, your ears and into you mind on a daily basis. No matter what the venue is, it's very convenient to get distracted and engulfed within the ideals and goals of being this or becoming that, but when it's time to turn some of those images off, and start living successfully and realistically at being yourself, you don't know how because all of what you know has been surrounded within the avenues of fantasy. Before you knew what was going on, the lines have become a blur, and you can't find your way out of wonderland.

So how are you supposed count up the cost of pursuing perfection? How do you keep from paying such a sacrificial price? When do you bring clarity, and redraw the lines between reality and fantasy so that you can come back from the wonderland experience? Well, you start by taking another step to realize and understand unattainable perfections.

Unattainable perfections are expectations that a woman has towards her own body, which is how so many women and girls are developing body dimorphic disorder—also known as BDD. Unattainable perfections are images that in reality are impossible to live and come up to. They are thoughts that you have towards yourself that put you in a place and a position to be hurt, angry, and ashamed, disappointed, and disgusted, with who you are, what you have, and what you look like. Unattainable perfections are when you strive to be someone or something that is contrary and opposes who you truly are. It's when you sacrifice your own identity to mask and perpetrate someone else's.

Unattainable perfections cause you to magnify what you think and perceive to be wrong, damaged, different ugly, disfigured, and distasteful about yourself. It changes your mindset and outlook, which causes you to lose confidence, focus, respect, and love for who you are. Last but not least, unattainable perfections are habits that create dangers and hazards toward your own life.

In all of these descriptions, I'm sure that there is something that you are able to identify with. In case there isn't, I'll sum up an unattainable perfection in two words: Skin Deep. What is skin deep? Skin deep is the stature upon which you make first impressions, analysis, conclusions, judgments, etc., about yourself and others. It is the measure, in which many women weigh and justify who they are, why they are, how much their worth, and how well they deserve to be treated by themselves and by others.

Skin deep is the way you present yourself to others by displaying who it is that you want people to see and believe about who you are. It's the basis upon which many women sell themselves to the world; whether it's in the marketplace, society, relationships, culture, or even self will. To simplify, skin deep is the depth of your outer woman. It's only what you can see with your eyes. And for most women, it is also the very limitation of what they will never discover within their heart.

So unattainable perfections are skin deep. They are the ones that you constantly change, but you can never get right. They do well for a season, but they are never permanent. They satisfy for a moment in time, but they do not quench an ever-increasing thirst to be right. No matter what you do, how you do it, or who you do it with, it seems as if you can never get that perfect fit. There's always something else that you can add to the equation to make yourself look and feel better.

What was once just a trip to the clinic, salon, tanning booth,

BODY IMAGE

etc., has now become a final destination. Instead of you driving by, you drop in. Slowly but surely you're seeing that you are loosing yourself within all of these endless pursuits. You may not be tired. You may not even care, but there is still something that you should know; and I want to make it crystal clear. So listen carefully.

Since you are uniquely made, it's important for you to make sure that you don't lower yourself in order to obtain something that isn't real. Stop trying to find uniqueness by being the same. What makes you, who you are, is your difference. You may not agree with that, and that's okay, but sooner or later, you will come to the understanding that what you see isn't always what you will get. When it all hits the fan, reality is the only thing that will be left uncut.

So let's face that reality. You will never find satisfaction in trying to become the image of perfection. Why? Because these cosmetics (no matter what kind they are) can be very convenient — even when you want to delude reality and shade the truth. When you try to create on the outside what's really missing on the inside, you end up doing more harm, than good — despite the gratification you receive. The truth is that sooner or later, you will get tired of beautifying the places where you hurt. You will get weary from your frustrations and worries, because you are afraid to talk about and discuss what's really going on.

You can't mascara pain, for the eyes are the windows of the soul. You cannot blush away anxiety and fear. You can't lipo unforgiveness or dye away the unknown. You can't botox your insecurities, or tan away your inner struggles and addictions. Yet in all of these things, we spend countless hours of our lives trying to conceal them, when in truth, we're actually trying to live up to an expectation that we do not understand. We put up with it anyhow. Not because we can't escape, but because we don't know that we have a choice to.

Whether you know it or not, you have a choice not to go to such extremes. You have a choice as to whether or not you want to have certain procedures done to your body. You deserve to have the option to choose and say no — it's not for me. Whatever your decision is, you have the responsibility to make sure that its right for you. You have the responsibility to do the proper research — not only in credentials, but in your own heart as well. Look well into your going, because there are many paths and ways that seem right, but the end thereof is nothing short of D.E.A.T.H. ((Disappointment, Exasperation, Anxiety, Turmoil, and Hate).

Therefore, you need to be careful not to become too fixated on your looks. Why? Because there are people who look good on the outside, but on the inside they are completely falling apart. Even though it's okay for you to make wishes and have dreams and desires about how you want to see yourself, you also have to make sure that in the midst of all of that, that you don't forget to look at yourself wholly. If you're only looking on the outside, then your only visualizing yourself skin deep. The truth is that there is more to you than what meets your eye.

You are an individual. You have individual features, shapes, sizes, wants, needs, desires, etc. This means that you can't be like the other woman. Why? Because who you are in this life it's all about balance. What's for you — is for you, and nobody else can have it but you. So you might as well be the only woman and the best woman that you can be — and that is YOURSELF; and guess what? When you start being yourself, you will find out that you were the "it" girl all along. You will finally see that you had all the right things, in all the right places the whole time. You'll discover that everything that you were in pursuit of, you already possessed — not because of what you added, but because of what you released.

The truth of the matter is that you do not live in a perfect world, even though Hollywood may make it look like it. So don't continue to jump stupid. Start thinking things through. Even though society tells you that it's all about what you do and how you look, you have to know that there is more to you than your appearance and what you do to keep up appearances. And that is where the rubber meets the road in the aspect of skin deep and unattainable perfections.

So stop trying to fit into Cinderella's shoe. Go and get fitted for your own. You are a perfect woman, and there is a perfect shoe that fits just right for you. How do I know? I know because there is no "one size fits all". There are just certain things that are just for you. And it's about time that you start looking — not from without, but from within.

Face-Off

Since the day woman was created, there has been something that has stalked her in the shadows. Like a tug of war, she has had to struggle and pull between the thin line of love and hate. In any instance, she can be persuaded to choose one side over the other, only to be tossed to and fro by the ever-changing tides of opinion and her emotions. No matter how great her strength or how strong her will, in the end her weaknesses continue to get the best of her. They are the grasps that keep her trapped within the four corners of a glass. Despite the many attempts to break free, her desperation to see her reflection has become the rope that keeps her tied to her past, her fears, her reality, and her pain.

Every day, she has the constant chore of pleasing the woman in the mirror. From the moment she sets foot into the bathroom, her labors are aimed for the acceptance and affirmation of the viewers. She lives her life on the basis of, "Will they like what they see", only to go out and experience the feelings of rejection and intolerance. So she resorts to the one that will never lie to see if she could ever become the fairest of them all. What she sees tells her no; for there is always one who is fairer than she.

Now all that she has seems worthless. All she can think about is how she can measure up to be someone who is worthy, accepted, and loved, but there is no amount of congeniality that can bring her to a permanent resolution, so that she can finally settle and have peace about who she is and the way she looks. All, of who she is, is now invested into a reflection — one that is a respect of persons. One that seems to magnify all of her imperfections, and minimize all of her attributes. There is now condemnation where there used to be confidence, and animosity where there used to be appreciation.

Instead of receiving and embracing the things that make her who she is, she focuses on the things and the places that she thinks are defective, insignificant, imperfect, and insufficient. She longs for the day when she can finally awake to see someone who she can be proud of — someone who she can rejoice and smile over. She longs to see the girl that she has imagined and sought after, to appear. Each and everyday she awaits the manifestation and reveal of the image that will forever change her life. But days turn into weeks, weeks to months, and months to years.

In her eyes that day never comes. It's just one disappointment after the other. She's tried everything in her power to make it happen, but each time she comes that much closer to attaining her goal, the finish line seems to move that much further out of her reach. For her, tomorrow never comes; and yesterday is too late. All she seems to have left is a shadow of a dream that never came to pass and a wish that hasn't been granted.

So she does what so many other women have done. She gives up. She loses hope, and she stops loving who she is. Her smile is still there, but so is the pain. Even though she still laughs until tears fall down her face, no one seems to know that those tears are real. In order for her to numb the pain and embarrassment, she keeps herself busy in the day to day routines and habits of everyday life. Even though she continues to function outwardly, in her heart and soul, she is dying.

She doesn't allow anyone else to see the hurt and frustrations that she carries within. They don't know that the only things that are keeping her going are the needs, demands, and wants of family, friends, school, work, etc. Although she presents herself well, nobody truly knows how hard it was for her to get out of bed and get herself fixed and ready just a few hours before. Sure, she looks okay, but in reality, she has already gone beyond her breaking point.

As story-like as this may sound, it is the life and reality of thousands of women; and pharmacies have the prescriptions to prove it. But the truth of the matter behind this billion-dollar issue is that none of us wants to be avoided. We all want to be accepted and included in something. We all want to have purpose, even if that purpose is to be sexy, noticed, attractive, and picture perfect. Even when we pretend as if it doesn't matter what others think and say about us, the truth is that, the majority of women and girls are spending their lives an their substance trying to be accepted. Everyday, we're trying to look the part, live the script, and dress the role that we cannot play. We continue to do it knowing that what we're doing doesn't even come close to who it is that we are as individuals.

So I have to ask: "Are you the girl that I'm describing?" Are you the young lady who has a love/hate relationship with yourself? Are you the one whose tears are real even though they are masked in laughter? Are you the one who's being tossed to and fro with emotions and opinions about the way you look? Are you the woman who can't seem to find your way back to your own heart? If you are, then I have something that I want to share with you.

There is hope for you. There is a way out. However, you're going to have to come out fighting. After all, this is a face off. This is the moment where you are going to step into the ring and make a decision as to which side you're going to stand on, because you're in the throws between imperfections versus self-acceptance. As crazy as that may sound, it's exactly what you need to hear.

The match between imperfection and self-acceptance is one that has been the anticipated event in every girl and woman's life. It's the main attraction that takes place every single day and for some of us, it's the nucleus upon which our entire lives are centered on. Whatever the case may be, it's time for you to gear up and face the woman in the mirror. Whether you go with tears in your eyes or rage in your heart, you have to enter in knowing that one way or the other, you're coming out victorious.

How do I know? I know because before there were mirrors, or pictures, there was a reflection. These reflections are what we all seem to base our worth on at some point and time. It's strange how your reflection makes you reevaluate who you are as a woman. Just like the numbers on the scale, what we see in the mirror has a very strong influence in how we go about our daily lives. Who would have thought that a simple reflective image would cause so much fury and uproar?

Now days, there are two categories of women. There are the ones who avoid mirrors altogether and there are ones who can't seem to stay away from them. However, there isn't a difference between the two, because they are both based in fear. The woman who avoids the mirror is afraid to see who she has become, and the woman who can't stay away is afraid to miss who she will evolve to be. Whichever you identify with, you have a common ground with every woman everywhere.

However, it is the fear of difference places us all in front of the mirror. It's what brings unjustified judgment and criticism. The fear of being different puts you in the position to be shunned by you, and it becomes the microscope that magnifies what you do and do not have. In truth, I don't know one woman who doesn't pick at herself. I don't know one single female who hasn't disliked something on her body. Whether it was her nose, her eyes, her hips, her legs, her ankles, her neck, her lips, her chin, her forehead, her ears, and the list goes on. That still isn't an excuse or good enough reason for you or any other woman to cast away her confidence and self-affirmation.

So I want you to ask yourself these questions: "What if there were no mirrors on the wall? What if there is only a canvas upon which you must sketch a projection of who you perceive yourself to be? What if you look into the window of your heart and see your true reflection? Or, would you even take an in depth looks, for fear of what you might discover?

Even though there are many portraits of the way you can see yourself, the reflection will still be the same. You can change everything about you, but you will still be you. You can even

BODY IMAGE

alter what you see and the way you see, but your eyes will never lie. You can smile a new smile, but your eyes will still display the truth that is in your heart—even with contacts. You can hold it all together, but in time, it will break loose.

Sooner or later you will have a showdown with yourself. The guns will be drawn, and your own worst enemy will be staring back at you with just as much hatred, anger, rage, and animosity as you have. It will have the same vengeance, just like you. This enemy will make every move that you make. And it will have the same ending as you. It's the face off that all of us come to. It isn't the battle of the bulge or the war of the scale. It's the apocalypse and Armageddon of you and your reflection.

This is where you will end, and where you will begin. It's where you will take your last and your first breath. This is where you will be buried and resurrected. It's judgment day. It's the day that you will stand before you, and be both defender and prosecutor. This is the day that you become both judge and jury as you plead your case before your reflection. This is the day that you will go on trial to fight for your captivity or your freedom. So do you swear to tell the truth, the whole truth, and nothing but the truth—so help you God?

Don't convict yourself to exile. It's not time for you to give up. The verdict is in your hands. Whatever you choose, I want you to know that I love you, despite of what you look like and what you do or do not have. Most importantly, you should love you, despite of all the things that are right, wrong, irregular, missing, bulging, uneven, or whatever the case may be.

When you have insecurities about yourself, your body, and

what you see in the mirror, then it's only a matter of time before you end up in a place of confusion. This is why it's so dangerous to have your self-esteem and your identity wrapped up in the image that's displayed before you. Every time you see yourself as lacking one thing, and having too much of another, you somehow end up in a never-ending story of like this, hate that, keep this, erase that. You should know that hating yourself won't get you anywhere in life, nor does it do you any good. You only have one life to live, and you can't live it in disgust because you hate who you are, what you look like, or what you do and do not have.

You have to love yourself despite what you see, because if you don't, who will? No one can love you like you love yourself. Whether you think it to be true or not, you being loved is not based on your worthiness or what you look like. If that were true, then none of us are worthy to be loved. You being loved is your God given right as a human being, an individual, and as a woman. But this is the catch: It has to come from within.

Now it's important for you to know that this will not happen over night. You have to continue to work at these things so that you can finally see yourself the right way. A way that doesn't beat you down, or tear you apart. So renew your mind because it's about time for you to see yourself for who you really are. Start being thankful for who you are and what you have. Why? Because who you are, is what makes you, you.

So move outside of self-criticism, and move into self-motivation and self-acceptance. When no one else will accept or affirm you, take the initiative, and accept and affirm yourself.

BODY IMAGE

You should no longer accept being afraid to be yourself. So next time you step into your bathroom, remember these words: "Mirror, mirror, on the wall, what you see is not who you are."

Get Flawed

It's every woman's desire to look and to feel beautiful. We want to have confidence in who we are as women and as individuals, knowing that we have what it takes to confront, compliment, and conqueror the world. We all search for the affirmation that reassures us and gives us a hope in knowing that in whatever we do, we are doing it successfully and righteously, but when we don't think or feel as if we have attained that level of beauty and confidence, somehow we end up with a kind of shame. The kind that follows us, and badgers us like a sixth sense. One that's filled with a measure of guilt, condemnation, and unworthiness to be alive and enjoy everyday life.

Regardless to our age, shape, size, stature, position, etc, each of us has a need to know that we have and possess the one thing that defines us as being women. Whether it's the perfect outfit, the right walk, or flawless makeup, there is an expectation that we have of ourselves to be beautiful. We exert such an anticipation to obtain the maximum level of beauty that it keeps us coming back for more. More acceptance, more confidence, more complements, more looks, more relationships, more opportunities, more respect, more attention, more happiness, more purpose, more satisfaction, more pleasure, more joy; and in general, just more out of life.

BODY IMAGE

We crave for ourselves the things that will make us stand out, stand tall, and stand strong. We deplete all of our resources whether — externally or internally to make sure that we have some kind of share or ownership in the economic trade of beauty; and all that it has to offer. It has become the scale that we weigh out worth on, and the measure by which we uphold a standard of entitlement. It's where we find our identity, our click, and our reason for existence. It tells us who we are, what we should have, what we deserve, and what we should dream, even to the point where it ends up being a place of infatuation.

The hidden clause in the contract of beauty that no one discussed when we signed on and bought in was that it will always be in the eye of the beholder. No one ever said that beauty is what you would make of it. This has ultimately left too many of women who have unwillingly or unknowingly fallen victim to the life of pleasing the beholder — even when it is just herself.

Beauty in today's culture has evolved into a cataract that is blinding the eyes of women so that they cannot see the truth in all that they've been created and purposed to be. As critical or judgmental as that may sound, it is true. However, it isn't the word that's the problem. It's the definition proceeding after the word that presents the issue and dilemma. How we women define beauty is what causes us to present and pursue it in our daily lives. It is our definition that backs the way we express the word and ourselves, even if it's in a way that isn't edifying or positive.

So what are you supposed to do? How are you supposed to

find your way back to the truth? How can you restore confidence in who you are? What can you do to regain your footing and become a victor over pleasing the eye of the beholder? How do you begin to see clearly so that you can get back to the simplicity of beauty? Well, the answer to these questions can be found when you make another step and begin to develop a healthy self-expression.

Self-expression is the communication or assertion of your personality, your opinion, your thoughts, your feelings, and your outward indications through conversation, behavior, activities, poetry, writings, paintings, dance, fashion, etc. It is the way you transmit your ideas, beliefs, and goals. It is also the means in which you may convey messages, commands, or information between people or places. In other words, self-expression is your way of presenting to the world who you are, and what you're about.

Self-expression is the forerunner of your character and your purpose in life. It tells a lot about you even if you haven't said anything; which in today's terms is called a first impression. Through the avenue of your self-expressions, judgments are made and conclusions are drawn, even if they aren't right or fair. Self-expression is a way that some people let it all hang out, or hold it all in. Either way, your self-expression determines the way others will see you and reveals the way that you see yourself.

The way that you see yourself is a direct result of what it is that you believe about who you are. Therefore, whatever it is that you believe about whom you are, is what you will eventually use to define beauty. So I have to ask, how do you define beauty? How do you use beauty to relay a positive or negative self-expression? What are the words that you believe and write in your heart about being beautiful?

In case you may or may not have an answer at the moment, I want to share something with you that might help you and realign your focus just a bit. Whether you now it or not, there is more than one definition of beauty. Some might say it's a pretty face or a statuesque figure. Others may say its vanity; and that may be true. However, there is more to this world than what you may presently know or even believe.

Beauty is all around you. It's in nature, it's in the atmosphere. It's in your environment. It's in a sweet melody, a picture, and even a song. Beauty can be found in the words of a poem or the drawing of a child hanging on the refrigerator. It's in your favorite scent and even your favorite food. Beauty is in the holidays and the four seasons of the year. It's even in a family pet. Beauty can be your personality. It can be your smile. It can even be in your voice. Beauty can be your character. It can be your laughter. Beauty can even be found in your tears.

Beauty is in your passion. It's in your heart and your mind. Beauty is in your emotions. It is in your relationships. It's in your walk. It's in the way you talk. Beauty can be in your habits. It can be in your routine. It can be in the style of your hair. Beauty is even in your choices, your decisions, and your actions. Beauty is in love. It's in charity. It's in giving. It is in compassion. Beauty is in peace. It's in serenity. It's in the cool of the day, and yes, beauty can even be found in death.

Beauty is in birth. It's even in labor. Beauty is what gives you hope, joy, and laughter. Beauty can be found in embarrassment, or on special occasions. Beauty is in your footsteps. It's in the moments that you cherish. Beauty is in time. It's in purpose, and it's in destiny. But there is one definition that speaks for all of these things. Beauty is what you make of it. It's how you perceive, imagine, and believe it to be. Even if you are the only one who sees it, it is still your very own self-expression—and that's important. That's why beauty is in the eye of the beholder.

No matter who backs you or agrees with you, your view is the right one. You have the absolute best seat in the house of your life and your body. If you don't believe me, here is a brief literary illustration that I want you to carefully consider. *In the winter, a tree can be considered to be barren and ugly. It's without the leaves that bring color and character in the spring and fall. It's without the shade from the noonday sun in the summer. When the wind blows there is no swaying of anything, accept hardened, cold, flawed, and seemingly lifeless branches. The tree almost looks dead and abandoned, but the snow that falls in that season will coat that very same tree and bring out a beauty that was previously unseen and forgotten. When the spring rolls around again, the buds of life show forth a hope and promise that just a season ago seemed too far-gone.*

So what does this have to do with you? Everything! We all go through barren seasons. We all experience times in our lives where beauty has seemed to have been replaced with ugly. We've all had those areas in life that become lifeless and forgotten. Each and every one of us knows what it's like to be in a dead place, where silence is the liveliest conversation that you

BODY IMAGE

have had all day, but this is not your end. You must learn from the tree that it's flawed and abandoned state is only for a season. It won't last always.

You have got to learn how to 'be', in and out of season. Regardless to whether or not someone agrees with you, it's your perception that truly matters. It's your vision that counts. No matter how flawed and unattractive you think you are in this season, whether it's in your body, your figure, your character, your emotions, your relationships, etc., you must be able to answer the inevitable question: "What do I see?"

Since beauty is in the eye of the beholder, you must learn how to find beauty in whatever season of life you're in. No one else should be allowed to encase, engulf, or degrade your splendor—not even you, but it's up all up to you. You alone must see who you are and know that you are the apple of God's eye. You need to know that you were fearfully and wonderfully made. "What does that mean?" It means that you have been selected and appointed to be a woman whose life will impact the world. What world is this? This is your world. It's everyday life.

This means that you must be able to enjoy everyday of your life just being you. Because who you are, is significant. You shouldn't just eat, but you need to enjoy what you're eating. You shouldn't just buy something because it fits, because it looks good, because it's hip and in style, or even because its name brand. You buy your wardrobe because it's what illuminates all of the things that make you, you. You need to look at yourself when you get out of the shower, so that you can see every inch and portion of your body; not glance and walk away.

Without comparison or competition, you need to know how to address and keep yourself according to the seasons of your life; fearing no judgment or criticism. Why? Because you are the beauty. You are the jewel. You are the priceless being that radiates elegance and splendor; not the things that you outwardly possess. Don't get me wrong, it's okay to wear clothing and have natural and luxurious things, but none of those things should be the entity of who you are. The clothing, the makeup, the nails, the shoes, the jewelry, or any accessory make you beautiful. In all actuality, they don't compliment you. You complement them. They don't complete you. You complete them. YOU are what bring beauty to any and all of these things.

It's okay to express yourself boldly, and in whatever way suits you best, but your expressions cannot be limited to one dimension. Just like an iceberg, so much of who you are is below the surface. That simply means that there are too many wonderful facets and manifolds to who you are and what you have, for you to only express them in one way. After all, beauty in its finest form is a matter of the heart, and that tells me that your beauty is limitless. So begin to develop a self-expression that is nurturing. One that will build you up positively in every area of your life and your body.

Start to surround yourself with people that will tell you the truth and support you in what you desire, envision, and dream to do and become. Because it's the metaphor of the tree that you will come upon a new season and a new day where you will blossom like never before, that life will be restored again. No matter what season of life you may be in, you are a woman whose beauty is beyond comparison.

So now is the time for your eyes to behold the beauty and splendor that is your life, and all that that means. So get flawed. Why? Because who you are and who you will become, is and will always be in the eye of the beholder. So go and behold the truth of whom you are; and that my friend, is BEAUTIFUL.

Get Real

A woman's body is her most prized possession. From the top of her head, to the soles of her feet, she will do anything and everything necessary to keep, maintain, and illuminate the areas and places of her body that will give her the perfect impression and presentation. From the time she awakes, everything that she does within that day will somehow revolve around what it is that she can do to make herself look better, feel better, weigh better, walk better, pose better, and last longer. Whether it's how many calories she will eat, how long she will spend at the gym, what treatment she'll undergo, or how much money she plans to spend on an outfit; she did it all in the name of her body.

However, despite of all of these things, she is still unsatisfied with who she is and what she looks like. But instead of her dealing with it, she finds something else to tickle her fancy and take her focus and attention off of the issue, while she continues to put on a show that will display the woman, whom everyone else wants, expects, receives and desires. It has turned into the pursuit for the highest achievement, and it's evolved into the glue that holds her together. Without any doubt or question, she just wants to fit in, but even with all of her efforts, trials, pledges, and restrictions, in her own heart and mind she still can't seem to make the cut.

BODY IMAGE

Now her body has become the tempest and storm to the sea of her thoughts, her feelings, and her emotions. She wants to have someone who will love, accept, affirm, and embrace the places on her body and in her life where she doesn't. Her body's image is now the lyric to the song of her life and the melody to the tune of her day. It has developed into a bridge of error, and fate that connects her to whom she is and who she dreams to be. Even after she has found the greatest sale, discovered the ultimate low calorie diet, developed the right routine, and made the desired weigh in, in the end it's still not enough to quiet the little voice inside her that says to her, "go a little further".

So she continues to do whatever is necessary to be reassured that what she has is good and not bad. She makes sure that who she presents to the world won't affect the way she is welcomed and received by the world. While at the same time, she is earnestly looking and searching for a place where she can feel safe and secure from abandonment, judgment, criticism, rejection, pain, abuse, and a number of other things. She no longer has a yearning to be original. Instead, she just desires to be the woman who everyone, including herself, will love, embrace, and appreciate; and in her mind, that's all that matters.

Now days, the constant stream of images and imaginations have completely impacted and affected the way she approaches who and what she is. For her, these influences have turned into unending efforts that are now her life's source and support, but at the same token, she keeps finding herself stuck within a parallel of to be and not to be. So she asks herself the same question that we all ask ourselves at one time or another: "Who am I?"

It is because of that question, that I now have to ask you: "Who is the real you?" No, not what you wear and put on, but who you truly are. What does your inner woman look like? Or have you even taken notice of yourself lately? If your eyes are the light of your body, then what's shinning from within you? Is there a bright array of life, or is there a faint glimmer of what used to be? Can you remember the last time that you were truly happy with whom you are, or has it been so long that you've forgotten what it's like to love being happy with you? Well, if you can't remember, then perhaps it's time for you to arise and shine — not from the outside in, but from the inside out. Maybe it's time for you take another step to create and establish an edifying self-image.

As women, we all share a common ground called self-image. It's the one where we weigh who we are by what we look like. However, very few of us have an edifying self-image, because too many of us are defining ourselves based on the reflection in the mirror, the numbers on the scale, the pictures in a magazine, or the attention from others. Self-image is an issue that we deal with on a regular basis, but when we leave it unguided or unadvised, it is also something that can become easily distorted and misinterpreted; which in turn changes the way we like and view ourselves. This can hinder us from unfolding and releasing our true self, because we feel unworthy, confused, angry, left out and cast aside.

This distorted self-image can be redefined as an identity

crisis, but for the sake of simplicity, it can also be described as the "ugly duckling" issue. Either way, it is still a point of controversy for every woman, where you may feel as if nobody likes you, wants you, needs you, desires you, understands you, hears you, or even seems to care or be aware that you're in a place of complete desperation and loneliness. No matter what you do, what you take, or who you're with, somehow you can't escape those thoughts that are running rapidly through your heart and mind that tell you that what you are feeling and seeing is true and cannot be changed. But I beg to differ.

When you begin to give your self-image a purpose that is beyond what you feel and what you see, you are then creating change because you are now establishing an edifying self-image. You are now cultivating a projection of yourself (your inner woman) that truthfully displays who you are — without guilt, condemnation, or compromise. When you are creating an edifying self-image, you're establishing a personal view of all of whom you are — spirit, soul, and body. It's what you are presenting before others that will convey to them what you believe about yourself and consequently what they will eventually begin to believe about you.

Having an edifying self-image means that you rightly possess an idea, concept, and mental image that compliments, graces, and affirms who you are. It states that what you have and who you are goes beyond all appearances and trends. It communicates that you know you are a woman who is radiant, magnificent, sexy and beautiful. It says that you are a woman of purpose, virtue, value, and elegance. Which in a nutshell simply means that you like who you are and what you see, and are unafraid and unashamed to first let yourself know it, and then to let the whole world know it.

Even when everyone is telling and showing you that the real you isn't good enough or worthy, an edifying self-image is the angel on your shoulder reminding you that they're the ones who are missing out on an extraordinary woman, individual, and human being. It establishes a foundation of confidence within you, declaring that you aren't anxious or worried about whether or not someone else sees what you see because you know and have assurance that what you see is already G.O.O.D. (Glorious, Outstanding, Original, and Distinguished)

So an edifying self-image helps you to understand that it's okay for you to stop trying to fit in. It lets you know that you don't have to continue to disguise yourself in a costume that deflects who you really are because who you are and what you have already has worth and value. Even though there is a lot being said out there about who, what, and how a woman should look and be, an edifying self-image becomes your guide and advisor that tells you to remember to take the time out to stop and ask yourself, "Is this right for me?" And it brings to your awareness the facts and fictions, the truths and flaws by saying that just because it's hip or popular, doesn't mean that it's right.

Even if it tops the list as the ten most important and seasonal things that you must have, it still doesn't signify or validate it as being right for you. In all truth, an edifying self-image relays to you that only you can determine what's right for you and what fits you best—not someone or something else. So be very careful

BODY IMAGE

that you don't lose your ability to think and choose for yourself. You can't let "things" determine your self-image or your identity, because your self-image directly reflects your identity, which is in itself, a value that can never be replaced.

Even when things and people around you make you feel as if you have nothing to offer or attribute, I want you to know that you do. This is exactly why you need to discover what's good about you and who you are. In fact, your life is proof that you have a reason and a purpose to be here. You have more to offer and attribute to the earth, others, society, community, etc. than you think you do. How do I know? I know because your life is a gift to all mankind.

The things that are on in the inside of you spell out greatness. Regardless to how you may look or what things may look like in your life, you should always remember that you are a woman whose life and purpose are a gift, a blessing, and a treasure to all. You should know that who you are is worth so much more than things, stuff, or anything anyone can offer. So who you are should not be measured in how much you weigh, what you wear, what size you are, or even who you know. Why? Because your edifying self-image reveals to you that who you are has no measure. It will teach you that there is nothing that this world has to offer you that can even come close to your uniqueness and radiance; and that is what makes you priceless.

I have to tell you that you are a woman whose life can never be replaced. You cannot be erased even if you wanted to, because there is too much about you that makes history and changes the course of time. How do I know? I know because there will never be another you. You are the only one, which means that you are making history everyday of your life. Everyday that you awake you are producing life changing events that no other people, past, present, or future will ever be able to compare to.

So don't continue to trash yourself by having a self-image that says things and causes you to wear things, or do things that diminish and deplete you. Why? Because if you were to get real and be completely honest with yourself, you already know that it has become a burden that you're not strong enough to bear. Even when you thought that it was going to be easier to be what everyone else said you should be, you know good and well that it's slowly killing you from the inside out. Just in case you don't believe that you could possibly be doing that to yourself, I want to challenge you to get real—really quickly.

If you make an effort to start looking for the things that are right about you, gradually, you will begin to see some changes that will redirect the way you perceive, address, and promote yourself. If you may not know how to look for what's right about you or where to begin, I'll give you a head start: You're here. You're breathing, you're blinking, and you have Life in your body. It may not be the life or body that you want, but you're certainly not without. You even have something that someone else may wish and pray that they could have. Whether you like it or not, there is something about you that someone else would die for—and has died for.

So don't beat yourself up anymore, because the real you is not what you see. It's who you are when nobody's looking.

Therefore, discover the uniqueness of you. Find out what it is that you possess that no one else can even compare or come close to. I dare you to take another look at yourself, but this time when you do it, take a look from the inside out. It's so much more defining and fulfilling when you do. Perhaps you may even uncover the hidden treasure that you have been searching for, for all this time. Wouldn't it be amazing for you to finally see yourself for the first time? Talk about liberation.

Now is the time for you to make the decision to create an edifying self-image. One that will show you how to love yourself in every season and area of your life. Don't allow yourself to worry any longer about the he said, she said. Start listening to what you say. After all, your words are the ones that matter, and make the most impact. Your words are what reveal what it is that you truly believe about yourself and your body.

So will the real you please stand up? Now I'm not asking you to put yourself on display for someone else's gratification. I'm asking you to stop shutting your own eyes to the beauty and splendor of who you are. You do have something to offer and add to this world. You have a value and worth that goes beyond accessories, fashion, fame, money, etc. Although it may be buried, hidden, and covered up, you do have a hidden treasure within you. It may take a little time and effort to uncover and unfold it, but in due season, it will come to pass. And when you grasp that, then will you understand that there is truly more to your life than what meets the eye.

Words from the Author

Although this may be the end of this book, it is not the end of your life. The last chapter didn't mark the last step. It simply implied that you have to keep walking. And that's the key to progress and change. You have to continue to take steps. Keep putting one foot in front of the other so that you can arrive at the place that you envisioned, planned, and purposed yourself to be. But if you stop taking those steps, then you stop moving forward. When you stop moving forward, backsliding is inevitable. So in case you didn't get anything that was written beforehand let me sum this entire book up in these words: Imperfections are apart of life: But they are also the true beauties of life, and the hardest test and challenge you will ever face in your life will be accepting those imperfections — which is why the love that you have for yourself should be unconditional and without limitations. Once you do, you'll finally come to a place where you will truly know and understand that accepting all of who you are is, and will always be you embracing your imperfections. In the end you will see that all of who you are means that you believe in who you can be and who you are destined to become.

Even when you may think that who you are and what you have is dead, dull, quivered, unpleasant, and unattractive, I'm here to let you know that in due season, you will spring forth and blossom. You may be in your coldest winter and your darkest night, but soon you will have beauty for ashes, the oil of joy for mourning, and the garment of praise for the spirit of heaviness. Your weeping may endure for a night, but joy will come in the morning. Your time of grief and desperation will end. You will come through the storm. You will pass through the valley of the shadow of death. Your destiny is not here in this place. You will come through triumphantly and victoriously. Your end is not yet. Your life isn't over.

Now you may find that hard to believe from where you are right now, but I see your tomorrow, and it's going to be better than today. Even though your change may not be sudden, you still must know that each and every step that you take is one step closer to victory, triumph, and freedom. You can make it. I know that you can. So I want to encourage you to keep walking out the steps that you have been given—even when it gets hard. Because in the end you will arrive at the place where you can truly say and believe with all your heart, "I made it!"